YouTube Success Blueprint: Unleashing Revenue Streams for Creators

Table of content

Chapter 1: Introduction

Welcome to the exciting world of YouTube, where creativity meets opportunity, and passion can transform into a lucrative career. In this opening chapter, we embark on a journey to explore the vast landscape of YouTube and the untapped potential it holds for creators like yourself.

The YouTube Landscape

YouTube is not just a video-sharing platform; it's a global community where individuals share their stories, talents, and expertise. From makeup tutorials to gaming commentary, educational content to entertainment, YouTube is a canvas for creators to express themselves and connect with audiences worldwide.

The Power of Passion

What sets successful YouTubers apart is their genuine passion for what they create. We'll delve into inspiring stories of creators who started with a simple desire to share their interests and, through dedication and creativity, turned their channels into thriving businesses. This section aims to ignite your passion and help you see the immense possibilities that await.

The Evolution of YouTube Success

As we embark on this exploration, we'll take a brief look at the evolution of YouTube success. The platform has evolved from a space for casual video sharing to a dynamic marketplace where content creators can build not only an audience but also a sustainable income. Understanding this evolution sets the stage for the strategies we'll delve into throughout the book.

What This Book Offers

Before we dive into the specifics of making money on YouTube, let's outline what you can expect from this book. We'll cover everything from understanding your audience and crafting compelling content to mastering monetization techniques and navigating the intricate landscape of YouTube policies.

Your Journey Begins

Whether you're a seasoned creator looking to enhance your revenue streams or a newcomer eager to make your mark, this book is designed to be your guide. It's not just about making money; it's about building a brand, connecting with an audience, and turning your passion into a sustainable and fulfilling career.

So, buckle up as we navigate the world of YouTube success together. The path to financial freedom and creative fulfillment awaits, and this book is your compass for the journey ahead.

Chapter 2: Understanding Your Audience

Now that we've set the stage for your YouTube journey, it's time to delve into a critical aspect of success on the platform: understanding your audience. Building a loyal and engaged viewership is not just about creating content; it's about forging a connection with those who consume it. In this chapter, we explore the art and science of audience understanding.

Defining Your Target Audience

Who are you creating content for? Understanding your target audience is fundamental to tailoring your content to meet their needs and preferences. We'll discuss strategies for identifying and defining your audience, exploring demographic factors, interests, and the problems your content can solve for them.

Connecting Through Content

Your content is your bridge to your audience. We'll delve into the importance of creating content that resonates emotionally and intellectually with your viewers. From storytelling techniques to finding your unique voice, we'll explore ways to forge a genuine connection through the screen.

Researching Audience Behavior

To truly understand your audience, you need to dive into the data. We'll explore tools and analytics available on YouTube that provide insights into viewer behavior. Understanding metrics like watch time, demographics, and viewer retention can empower you to make informed decisions about your content strategy.

Engaging with Your Community

YouTube is more than just a content platform; it's a community. We'll discuss the significance of engaging with your audience through comments, polls, and social media. Building a sense of community around your channel not only strengthens your relationship with viewers but also enhances the discoverability of your content.

Feedback and Iteration

Feedback is a valuable resource on YouTube. We'll explore how to gather and interpret feedback from your audience, using it to iterate and improve your content. Whether through direct comments, surveys, or social media interactions, understanding what your audience enjoys and wants more of is key to sustained success.

Case Studies in Audience Connection

Drawing inspiration from successful YouTubers, we'll examine case studies of creators who have mastered the art of audience connection. These stories will offer practical insights into building a dedicated fan base and the positive impact it can have on your channel's growth.

Your Audience, Your Success

In essence, your audience is the heartbeat of your YouTube channel. Understanding who they are, what they seek, and how to engage with them is the foundation upon which we build the strategies for financial success on YouTube. As we move forward, remember: your audience is not just viewers; they're your community, and they play a vital role in your journey to YouTube success.

Chapter 3: Crafting a Compelling Content Strategy

Now that we've established the importance of understanding your audience, let's dive into the heart of your YouTube success: crafting a compelling content strategy. Your strategy is the roadmap that guides your content creation, helping you consistently deliver value to your audience and stand out in the crowded digital landscape.

Defining Your Content Niche

One of the keys to success on YouTube is finding and refining your content niche. We'll explore how to identify topics that align with your interests, expertise, and audience preferences. Whether you're passionate about technology, beauty, gaming, or educational content, honing in on your niche is crucial for building a dedicated viewership.

Planning Your Content Calendar

Consistency is the backbone of a successful YouTube channel. We'll discuss the importance of creating a content calendar to maintain a regular posting schedule. A well-planned calendar not only helps you stay organized but also keeps your audience engaged by providing them with a reliable stream of content.

Balancing Evergreen and Trending Content

A successful content strategy strikes a balance between evergreen content that remains relevant over time and trending content that capitalizes on current interests. We'll explore how to incorporate both types of content into your plan, ensuring a dynamic and appealing channel that caters to different viewer needs.

Storytelling Techniques for Impact

Great content goes beyond information; it tells a story. We'll delve into storytelling techniques that captivate your audience, create emotional connections, and leave a lasting impression. Whether you're creating educational tutorials or entertaining vlogs, weaving a narrative enhances the viewer experience.

Leveraging Multiple Content Formats

YouTube supports a variety of content formats, from traditional videos to live streams and shorts. We'll explore the advantages of each format and discuss how strategically incorporating them into your content strategy can broaden your reach and appeal to different audience segments.

Collaborations and Cross-Promotions

Collaborating with other creators is a powerful way to diversify your content and reach new audiences. We'll discuss the benefits of collaborations and provide insights into how to identify potential partners, initiate collaborations, and cross-promote content effectively.

Analytics-Driven Content Optimization

Your YouTube analytics are a goldmine of information. We'll explore how to interpret key metrics such as watch time, click-through rates, and audience retention. This data-driven approach allows you to optimize your content strategy continuously, ensuring you deliver what your audience values most.

Adapting to Trends and Challenges

The digital landscape evolves, and successful creators stay adaptable. We'll discuss strategies for staying informed about industry trends, adapting to algorithm changes, and navigating challenges that may arise on your YouTube journey.

Realizing Your Creative Vision

Crafting a compelling content strategy is not just about algorithms and metrics; it's about expressing your unique creative vision. We'll explore how to maintain authenticity while strategically aligning your content with audience interests and platform trends.

Your Content, Your Brand

In essence, your content is the vehicle through which you communicate with your audience. Crafting a compelling content strategy isn't just about gaining views; it's about building your brand and leaving a lasting impact. As we move forward, keep in mind that each piece of content is an opportunity to connect, inspire, and build the success you envision on YouTube.

Chapter 4: Monetization Basics

Now that we've laid the groundwork with an understanding of your audience and a compelling content strategy, it's time to explore the various avenues for turning your passion into profit on YouTube. In this chapter, we'll delve into the fundamental principles and strategies of monetization.

Introduction to Monetization

We'll start by unraveling the concept of monetization on YouTube. From the traditional AdSense program to newer features like Super Chat and channel memberships, we'll provide an overview of the diverse ways creators can generate revenue from their content.

AdSense and Beyond

AdSense is the entry point for many YouTubers looking to monetize their videos through ad revenue. We'll explore the basics of AdSense, how it works, and tips for optimizing your videos to maximize earnings. Additionally, we'll discuss the potential limitations and the importance of diversifying income streams.

Sponsorships and Brand Deals

Beyond AdSense, sponsorships and brand deals offer creators opportunities for lucrative partnerships. We'll guide you through the process of attracting and negotiating with sponsors, ensuring that collaborations align with your brand and provide value to your audience.

Affiliate Marketing Strategies

Affiliate marketing is a powerful monetization method that involves promoting products and earning a commission on sales. We'll discuss how to strategically incorporate affiliate marketing into your content, selecting products relevant to your audience and maintaining transparency in your promotions.

Merchandise Sales and E-Commerce

Diversifying your revenue streams is key to financial stability. We'll explore the world of merchandise sales and e-commerce, guiding you through the process of creating and promoting your own branded products. From custom merchandise to digital products, we'll cover the range of options available.

Channel Memberships and Premium Content

YouTube offers features like channel memberships and premium content for creators to provide exclusive perks to their audience. We'll delve into the strategies for implementing these features, building a loyal subscriber base, and offering premium content that adds value to your audience.

Maximizing Revenue with Fan Funding

Fan funding, often facilitated through features like Super Chat and YouTube Live, allows viewers to support creators directly. We'll discuss best practices for engaging your audience during live streams and optimizing fan funding options to boost your income.

Understanding YouTube's Monetization Policies

While the potential for revenue on YouTube is vast, creators must adhere to platform guidelines. We'll provide an overview of YouTube's monetization policies, including eligibility requirements and best practices to ensure compliance and ongoing monetization opportunities.

Balancing Monetization and Audience Experience

Successfully monetizing your channel requires a delicate balance between earning revenue and maintaining a positive viewer experience. We'll explore strategies for integrating monetization methods seamlessly into your content, ensuring that your audience feels valued rather than overwhelmed by promotional elements.

Setting Realistic Monetization Goals

Monetization success doesn't happen overnight. We'll discuss how to set realistic and achievable monetization goals, understanding that building a sustainable income on YouTube is a gradual process that requires dedication, consistency, and adaptability.

Your Journey to Monetization Mastery

As we conclude this chapter, remember that monetization is not a one-size-fits-all endeavor. Each creator's journey is unique, and the key is to experiment, learn from experiences, and adapt strategies based on what resonates with both your content and your audience. With a solid understanding of monetization basics, you're well-equipped to embark on the next phase of your YouTube journey.

Chapter 5: Building and Monetizing a Brand

With a firm grasp on your audience and a well-crafted content strategy, it's time to delve into the essential aspect of building a brand on YouTube. Your brand is more than just a logo or channel name; it's the identity that distinguishes you in the vast digital landscape. In this chapter, we'll explore how to establish and monetize a brand that resonates with your audience.

The Importance of Branding

Understanding the significance of branding is the first step. We'll delve into how a strong brand identity sets the tone for your content, fosters recognition, and helps you stand out in a sea of creators. We'll explore successful examples of YouTubers who have effectively built and leveraged their brands.

Defining Your Brand Identity

Your brand identity encompasses everything from your visual elements to your tone and values. We'll guide you through the process of defining your brand identity, including creating a memorable logo, selecting a consistent color palette, and establishing a unique voice that aligns with your content.

Creating a Cohesive Visual Style

Visual consistency is crucial for brand recognition. We'll discuss the importance of maintaining a cohesive visual style across your thumbnails, banners, and videos.

Tips for designing eye-catching visuals that reflect your brand's personality will be covered in detail.

Crafting an Engaging Channel Trailer

Your channel trailer is often the first impression viewers have of your brand. We'll explore strategies for creating an engaging and compelling channel trailer that effectively communicates your brand message and encourages viewers to subscribe.

Effective Brand Communication

Communication is at the heart of brand building. We'll discuss how to communicate with your audience consistently across all touchpoints, including video descriptions, social media, and community posts. Maintaining a transparent and authentic dialogue fosters a sense of connection and trust.

Leveraging Social Media for Brand Promotion

Social media platforms are powerful tools for extending the reach of your brand beyond YouTube. We'll explore strategies for effectively using platforms like Instagram, Twitter, and Facebook to promote your content, engage with your audience, and attract new viewers.

Monetizing Brand Partnerships

As your brand gains recognition, opportunities for partnerships and collaborations will arise. We'll discuss how to monetize brand partnerships, negotiating fair deals, and ensuring that collaborations align with your brand values while providing value to your audience.

Building a Brand Website and Email List

Taking your brand beyond YouTube involves establishing a presence outside the platform. We'll explore the benefits of creating a brand website and building an email list. These assets not only provide additional monetization opportunities but also serve as valuable tools for audience retention.

Protecting Your Brand: Copyright and Trademarks

Brand protection is a critical aspect of long-term success. We'll discuss the importance of understanding copyright and trademark laws, ensuring that your brand remains secure and legally protected as it grows.

Scaling Your Brand for Long-Term Success

Building a brand is an ongoing process of evolution. We'll explore strategies for scaling your brand over time, adapting to changes in your content, audience, and industry trends. Consistent brand evaluation and refinement are key to maintaining relevance and long-term success.

Monetization Opportunities Within Your Brand

As your brand gains traction, monetization opportunities multiply. We'll explore how a strong brand can open doors to merchandise sales, sponsored content, and even your own products or services. The culmination of effective branding is a brand that not only resonates with your audience but also contributes to your financial success on YouTube.

Your Brand, Your Success

In conclusion, your brand is the heartbeat of your YouTube presence. It's not just about recognition; it's about creating a meaningful connection with your audience. As you continue to refine and strengthen your brand, you're not only enhancing your influence but also unlocking additional avenues for monetization that align with your brand's values and your audience's needs. The journey to building and monetizing a brand is an exciting and dynamic process, and this chapter provides the foundation for your brand's growth and success on YouTube.

Chapter 6: Optimizing Videos for Search

Now that your brand is established, it's time to ensure that your content reaches its intended audience by mastering the art of search optimization. In this chapter, we'll explore the strategies and techniques to enhance the discoverability of your videos on YouTube, maximizing your reach and attracting a broader audience.

Understanding the Importance of Video SEO

Search Engine Optimization (SEO) is a game-changer for content creators. We'll delve into why video SEO matters on YouTube, how it impacts your video's visibility in search results, and its role in attracting organic traffic to your channel.

Keyword Research and Selection

Keywords are the foundation of video SEO. We'll explore how to conduct thorough keyword research to identify terms and phrases relevant to your content. Selecting the right keywords helps your videos surface in search results when users are actively looking for content like yours.

Strategic Placement of Keywords

Knowing your keywords is just the beginning. We'll discuss the strategic placement of keywords in your video title, description, and tags. Crafting compelling titles and descriptions that not only include relevant keywords but also entice viewers is crucial for maximizing click-through rates.

Creating Compelling Thumbnails

Thumbnails are the first visual impression viewers have of your video in search results. We'll explore strategies for creating eye-catching thumbnails that not only reflect your brand but also encourage users to click on your content amidst a sea of search results.

Optimizing Video Descriptions for Engagement

Your video description is a valuable real estate for providing additional information and context. We'll discuss how to optimize video descriptions to engage viewers, encourage them to interact with your content, and improve your video's overall search performance.

Utilizing Tags Effectively

Tags play a role in helping YouTube understand the context of your video. We'll explore best practices for selecting and using tags effectively. Properly chosen tags can improve your video's discoverability and association with related content.

Captivating Introductions for Viewer Retention

Viewer retention is a crucial factor in YouTube's algorithm. We'll discuss the importance of captivating introductions that hook viewers from the start. A strong beginning not only enhances viewer retention but also contributes to improved search rankings.

Creating Playlists for Increased Visibility

Playlists are an often-overlooked tool for optimizing your content. We'll explore how to create playlists strategically, grouping related videos together. Playlists not only enhance viewer experience but also contribute to increased visibility in search and suggested video recommendations.

Engaging with Viewers in Comments

YouTube values engagement, and comments are a significant metric. We'll discuss the importance of engaging with your audience through comments, how it contributes to search rankings, and strategies for fostering a positive and active community around your content.

Utilizing End Screens and Cards

End screens and cards provide opportunities to keep viewers engaged with your content. We'll explore how to strategically use end screens and cards to promote additional videos, playlists, and encourage viewers to subscribe, contributing to increased visibility in search results.

Monitoring Analytics for Continuous Improvement

Analytics are your compass in the world of YouTube SEO. We'll discuss how to interpret key metrics, such as watch time, click-through rates, and traffic sources. Regularly monitoring analytics allows you to refine your strategies, ensuring your content remains optimized for search performance.

Staying Updated on Algorithm Changes

YouTube's algorithm evolves, impacting search rankings and discoverability. We'll explore strategies for staying updated on algorithm changes, adapting your content strategy accordingly, and maintaining a proactive approach to SEO.

Internationalization and Multilingual SEO

Expanding your reach globally involves considerations for internationalization and multilingual SEO. We'll discuss how to optimize your videos for different languages, ensuring your content resonates with diverse audiences around the world.

Your Video, Their Search Journey

In conclusion, optimizing your videos for search is not just about algorithms; it's about understanding the journey of your potential viewers. By strategically incorporating keywords, engaging thumbnails, and fostering viewer interaction, you're not only improving your video's search performance but also creating a seamless and enjoyable experience for your audience. As you master the art of video SEO, you're positioning your content to be discovered by the right audience, ultimately contributing to the sustained success of your YouTube channel.

Chapter 7: Audience Engagement Strategies

With your content optimized for search, the next critical step in building a successful YouTube channel is fostering meaningful connections with your audience. In this chapter, we'll explore a range of strategies to boost audience engagement, creating a loyal community around your content.

The Power of Audience Engagement

Engagement is the lifeblood of a thriving YouTube channel. We'll start by discussing why audience engagement matters, how it impacts your channel's performance, and the role it plays in building a strong and dedicated community.

Responding to Comments Effectively

Comments are a direct line of communication with your audience. We'll explore strategies for responding to comments effectively, fostering positive interactions, and creating a sense of community within your comment section.

Encouraging Likes, Shares, and Subscriptions

Likes, shares, and subscriptions are valuable indicators of audience appreciation. We'll discuss techniques for encouraging these actions, including calls-to-action within your videos, end screens, and engaging with your audience through other platforms.

Hosting Live Q&A Sessions and Interactions

Live sessions provide a dynamic way to interact with your audience in real-time. We'll explore the benefits of hosting live Q&A sessions, responding to viewer questions, and utilizing features like Super Chat to enhance audience engagement.

Running Contests and Giveaways

Contests and giveaways can inject excitement into your channel and encourage audience participation. We'll discuss how to run engaging contests, set clear rules, and leverage partnerships to amplify the impact of your giveaways.

Creating Polls and Surveys

Polls and surveys are valuable tools for understanding your audience's preferences and gathering feedback. We'll explore how to use these features effectively on YouTube and other social media platforms to involve your audience in decision-making processes.

Showcasing Viewer Contributions and Shoutouts

Recognizing and showcasing viewer contributions is a powerful way to make your audience feel valued. We'll discuss how to incorporate shoutouts, feature user-generated content, and celebrate milestones together with your community.

Collaborating with Your Audience

Empowering your audience to contribute to your content creates a sense of co-creation. We'll explore ways to collaborate with your audience, whether it's through video ideas, challenges, or interactive elements that involve them in your creative process.

Encouraging Community Discussions

Community discussions can extend beyond the video comments. We'll discuss strategies for fostering discussions on community tabs, social media, and other platforms, creating a space where your audience can connect with each other.

Utilizing Social Media for Engagement

Social media platforms offer additional avenues for engagement. We'll explore how to strategically use platforms like Instagram, Twitter, and Facebook to complement your YouTube content, promote discussions, and connect with your audience in diverse ways.

Implementing Interactive Elements in Videos

Interactive elements within your videos can enhance engagement. We'll discuss how to use features like clickable annotations, cards, and end screens strategically to guide viewers to other content and keep them actively engaged.

Hosting Virtual Events and Meetups

Virtual events and meetups provide opportunities to connect with your audience on a deeper level. We'll explore how to organize virtual events, whether they're live-streamed Q&A sessions, virtual hangouts, or collaborative projects with your community.

Monitoring Analytics for Engagement Insights

Analytics aren't just for tracking views; they also provide insights into audience engagement. We'll discuss key metrics such as likes, comments, and watch time, and how to use this data to gauge audience interest and refine your engagement strategies.

Encouraging Constructive Feedback

Constructive feedback is invaluable for growth. We'll explore how to encourage your audience to provide feedback in a constructive manner, creating an environment where both positive and constructive comments are welcome.

Your Audience, Your Collaborators

In conclusion, your audience is more than viewers; they are collaborators in your creative journey. As you implement strategies to boost audience engagement, you're not just building numbers; you're fostering a community that actively contributes to the success of your channel. The journey to a highly engaged audience involves ongoing communication, collaboration, and a genuine appreciation for the individuals who make your content meaningful. As you continue to strengthen these connections, you're laying the foundation for a YouTube channel that not only grows but thrives through the active participation of your dedicated community.

Chapter 8: Collaborations and Partnerships

Collaborations and partnerships are powerful drivers for growth on YouTube. In this chapter, we'll explore the benefits of working with other creators, how to identify suitable collaborators, and strategies for successful partnerships that not only expand your audience but also enhance the overall content on your channel.

Understanding the Power of Collaborations

Collaborations are a cornerstone of YouTube success. We'll begin by exploring why collaborations are essential, the mutual benefits they offer to both collaborators, and the potential for reaching new audiences through shared content.

Identifying Compatible Collaborators

Not all collaborations are created equal. We'll discuss how to identify collaborators whose content aligns with yours, ensuring a seamless integration that appeals to both your existing audience and the audience of your collaborator.

Reaching Out and Initiating Collaborations

Initiating collaborations requires effective communication. We'll explore strategies for reaching out to potential collaborators, crafting compelling collaboration proposals, and building a network within your niche or community.

Planning and Executing Collaborative Projects

The success of a collaboration lies in careful planning. We'll discuss the importance of outlining clear objectives, defining roles, and establishing a timeline for collaborative projects. Whether it's a joint video, a series, or a cross-promotion initiative, strategic planning is key.

Leveraging Each Other's Audiences

Collaborations provide an opportunity to tap into each other's audiences. We'll explore strategies for cross-promotion, where both collaborators actively encourage their viewers to explore the content of the other, fostering mutual growth.

Utilizing Multi-Channel Networks (MCNs)

Multi-Channel Networks (MCNs) can facilitate collaborations and provide additional resources for creators. We'll discuss the benefits and considerations of joining an MCN, as well as how to navigate these partnerships effectively.

Navigating Challenges in Collaborations

While collaborations can be immensely rewarding, challenges may arise. We'll discuss common challenges in collaborations, such as differences in work styles or creative visions, and strategies for addressing these challenges constructively.

Analyzing Metrics and Measuring Collaboration Success

Measuring the success of a collaboration involves more than just view counts. We'll explore key metrics to analyze, including subscriber growth, audience engagement, and the impact on your channel's overall performance.

Case Studies in Successful Collaborations

Drawing inspiration from real-life examples, we'll explore case studies of successful collaborations. These stories will provide insights into what makes a collaboration effective and how creators can leverage partnerships for long-term success.

Building Long-Term Collaborative Relationships

One collaboration can lead to many more. We'll discuss how to build long-term collaborative relationships, creating a network of creators who support each other's growth and contribute to a thriving community.

Diversifying Collaboration Formats

Collaborations come in various forms. We'll explore different collaboration formats, including joint videos, interviews, challenges, and group projects. Diversifying collaboration formats keeps your content fresh and offers unique value to your audience.

Collaborating Across Different Niches

Venturing beyond your niche can open new doors for collaborations. We'll discuss the benefits and challenges of collaborating across different niches, and how these collaborations can introduce your content to diverse and untapped audiences.

Staying Authentic in Collaborations

Maintaining authenticity in collaborations is crucial. We'll explore how to stay true to your brand while collaborating with others, ensuring that the content resonates with your existing audience and contributes positively to your channel's identity.

Fostering a Collaborative Community

Collaborations extend beyond individual projects. We'll discuss how to foster a collaborative community within your niche or industry, creating a supportive environment where creators share resources, ideas, and opportunities.

Your Collaborative Journey Continues

In conclusion, collaborations are not just a means to an end; they're a journey of mutual growth and creativity. As you navigate the world of collaborations and partnerships, remember that each collaboration is an opportunity to learn, expand your horizons, and create content that resonates with a broader audience. By fostering genuine connections with fellow creators, you're not only enhancing your own channel but contributing to the dynamic and collaborative spirit of the YouTube community.

Chapter 9: Leveraging Analytics for Growth

Analytics are the compass that guides your YouTube journey. In this chapter, we'll explore the wealth of data available to you, how to interpret key metrics, and strategies for leveraging analytics to refine your content, enhance audience engagement, and drive continuous growth on your channel.

Understanding the Importance of Analytics

Analytics are more than just numbers; they provide insights into how your audience interacts with your content. We'll start by exploring why analytics are crucial for your channel's growth and how they can inform strategic decision-making.

Key Metrics: Views, Watch Time, and Click-Through Rates

Views, watch time, and click-through rates are foundational metrics. We'll delve into what these metrics signify, how they impact your channel's performance, and strategies for improving each to drive overall growth.

Audience Retention and Engagement Metrics

Viewer retention and engagement metrics offer insights into how audiences respond to your content. We'll discuss the significance of keeping viewers engaged throughout your videos and strategies for improving audience retention rates.

Demographic Insights and Viewer Location

Understanding your audience demographic is essential for tailoring your content. We'll explore how to interpret demographic insights, including age, gender, and geographic location, to create content that resonates with your specific viewer base.

Traffic Sources and Search Insights

Knowing where your viewers come from is key to optimizing your content distribution. We'll discuss the significance of traffic sources, including search, suggested videos, and external platforms, and how to use this data to refine your promotional strategies.

Device and Playback Metrics

Different devices and playback platforms impact user experience. We'll explore how to analyze device and playback metrics to ensure your content is optimized for various platforms, contributing to a seamless viewer experience.

Conversion Tracking for Monetization Goals

For those focused on monetization, conversion tracking is crucial. We'll discuss how to set and track conversion goals, whether it's increasing subscribers, driving merchandise sales, or encouraging audience participation in other revenue-generating activities.

Comparing Video Performance and A/B Testing

Comparing the performance of different videos provides insights into what resonates with your audience. We'll explore A/B testing strategies, including experimenting with thumbnails, titles, and content formats to refine your approach based on viewer preferences.

Utilizing YouTube Studio and External Analytics Tools

YouTube Studio is a powerful tool for creators, and external analytics tools can provide additional insights. We'll discuss how to navigate YouTube Studio effectively and explore external tools that can complement your analytics strategy.

Setting and Evaluating Goals

Setting clear goals is essential for growth. We'll discuss how to establish realistic and measurable goals for your channel, whether it's increasing subscribers, watch time, or diversifying income streams, and how to evaluate progress against these objectives.

Creating Actionable Insights from Analytics

Analytics should inform actionable insights. We'll explore how to extract meaningful takeaways from your analytics data, turning insights into practical strategies for content improvement, audience engagement, and overall channel growth.

Regularly Reviewing and Adapting Strategies

The digital landscape is dynamic, and strategies must evolve. We'll discuss the importance of regularly reviewing your analytics, staying informed about industry trends, and adapting your content and promotional strategies to align with changing viewer behaviors.

Engaging with Your Community Through Analytics

Sharing insights with your audience fosters transparency and community engagement. We'll explore how to communicate key analytics findings with your audience, whether through community posts, live Q&A sessions, or dedicated analytics-related content.

Staying Compliant with YouTube Policies

Certain analytics practices may have implications for privacy and compliance. We'll discuss the importance of adhering to YouTube's policies and guidelines when collecting and sharing analytics data, ensuring ethical and responsible use.

Your Analytics-Driven Growth Journey

In conclusion, analytics are not just a tool for tracking; they are a catalyst for growth. As you navigate the wealth of data available to you, remember that each metric tells a story about your audience, content performance, and the overall health of your channel. By embracing a data-driven approach, you're not only refining your content and strategies but also creating a channel that continually evolves and resonates with your audience. Your analytics-driven growth journey is a dynamic and ongoing process, and with each insight gained, you're positioning yourself for sustained success on YouTube.

Chapter 10: Navigating Challenges and Staying Resilient

Success on YouTube is a journey filled with highs and lows. In this chapter, we'll explore common challenges that creators face, strategies for overcoming setbacks, and how to cultivate resilience to ensure your long-term success on the platform.

Embracing the Rollercoaster of Creator Life

The life of a content creator is dynamic, with both triumphs and challenges. We'll start by acknowledging the highs and lows of the journey, from viral successes to periods of slower growth, and how to maintain a balanced perspective through it all.

Dealing with Algorithm Changes

YouTube's algorithm is ever-evolving, and changes can impact your channel's performance. We'll discuss strategies for staying informed about algorithm updates, adapting your content strategy, and mitigating the effects of algorithmic shifts.

Managing Burnout and Creative Blocks

Consistent content creation can lead to burnout and creative blocks. We'll explore techniques for managing stress, maintaining a healthy work-life balance, and reigniting your creative spark when faced with challenges.

Handling Negative Feedback and Criticism

Negative feedback is inevitable, but how you handle it shapes your journey. We'll discuss strategies for dealing with criticism, separating constructive feedback from trolls, and turning negative experiences into opportunities for growth.

Adapting to Changes in Trends and Audience Preferences

Trends and audience preferences can change rapidly. We'll explore how to stay attuned to shifts in your niche, adapt your content to evolving trends, and maintain relevance with your audience over the long term.

Navigating Copyright and Content ID Issues

Copyright claims and Content ID issues are common challenges on YouTube. We'll discuss how to navigate these situations, understand fair use principles, and protect your content from unwarranted claims.

Overcoming Plateaus in Growth

Plateaus in growth are natural, but they can be discouraging. We'll explore strategies for overcoming growth plateaus, reevaluating your content strategy, and identifying new opportunities to revitalize your channel.

Diversifying Income Streams for Financial Stability

Over-reliance on a single income stream can be risky. We'll discuss the importance of diversifying your revenue streams, exploring new monetization avenues, and building a resilient financial model for sustained success.

Maintaining Consistency During Life Changes

Life changes can impact your ability to create content consistently. We'll explore strategies for maintaining consistency during life events, managing expectations with your audience, and incorporating flexibility into your content schedule.

Building a Support System Within the Creator Community

The creator community can be a source of support. We'll discuss the importance of building relationships with fellow creators, sharing experiences, and creating a support system to navigate challenges collectively.

Strategies for Channel Rebranding and Reinvention

Rebranding or reinventing your channel may become necessary. We'll explore strategies for successfully executing a channel rebrand, including communicating changes to your audience and aligning your content with the new direction.

Staying Adaptable in a Dynamic Landscape

Adaptability is a creator's greatest asset. We'll discuss the mindset of staying adaptable, being open to experimentation, and embracing change as a natural part of the evolving landscape of online content creation.

Celebrating Milestones and Successes

Amidst challenges, it's essential to celebrate milestones and successes. We'll explore the importance of acknowledging your achievements, expressing gratitude to your audience, and finding joy in the journey.

Cultivating Resilience for Long-Term Success

Resilience is the key to long-term success. We'll discuss how to cultivate resilience, develop a growth mindset, and view challenges as opportunities for learning and improvement, ensuring that you emerge stronger from every setback.

Your Journey, Your Legacy

In conclusion, your journey as a content creator is unique, filled with lessons, growth, and an ever-expanding tapestry of experiences. Navigating challenges is not just a part of the process; it's an opportunity for resilience, adaptation, and ultimately, for creating a lasting legacy on YouTube. As you embrace the twists and turns of your creator journey, remember that each challenge is a stepping stone towards your goals, and your ability to overcome them is a testament to your strength and dedication as a content creator.

Chapter 11: Future Trends and Evolving Strategies

The digital landscape is ever-changing, and successful creators stay ahead by anticipating future trends and adapting their strategies. In this chapter, we'll explore emerging trends, technological shifts, and strategies for staying relevant as you navigate the evolving world of online content creation.

Embracing Emerging Content Formats

New content formats continually emerge on digital platforms. We'll explore the latest trends, such as short-form videos, interactive content, and virtual reality experiences, and discuss how creators can embrace these formats to engage audiences in innovative ways.

Understanding the Impact of Technology on Content Creation

Advancements in technology shape the content creation landscape. We'll discuss the impact of technologies like artificial intelligence, augmented reality, and immersive media on content creation, as well as how creators can leverage these tools to enhance their content.

The Rise of Niche Communities and Micro-Influencers

Niche communities and micro-influencers are gaining prominence. We'll explore the power of building niche communities, the influence of micro-creators, and strategies for creators to connect with specific audiences in meaningful ways.

Navigating the Evolution of Social Media Platforms

Social media platforms are dynamic, with features and user behaviors evolving over time. We'll discuss strategies for staying updated on platform changes, adapting your content for different platforms, and navigating the shifting landscape of social media.

The Growing Importance of Sustainability and Social Impact

Audiences are increasingly conscious of sustainability and social impact. We'll explore how creators can align their content with social and environmental values, contributing to positive change and resonating with audiences who prioritize ethical considerations.

Exploring Virtual and Augmented Reality Experiences

Virtual and augmented reality experiences are becoming more accessible. We'll discuss the potential of VR and AR for content creation, from immersive storytelling to virtual events, and how creators can explore these technologies to enhance viewer engagement.

Globalization and Connecting with Diverse Audiences

The internet has made content creation a global endeavor. We'll explore strategies for connecting with diverse audiences worldwide, including considerations for cultural sensitivity, language localization, and creating content that transcends geographical boundaries.

The Continued Rise of Educational and Tutorial Content

Educational and tutorial content remains highly popular. We'll discuss the enduring appeal of content that informs and educates, explore emerging trends in online learning, and provide strategies for creators to deliver valuable educational experiences.

Interactive and Community-Driven Content

Audiences crave interactivity and community engagement. We'll explore the rise of interactive content, including live streaming, polls, and community features, and discuss strategies for fostering a sense of community and active participation around your content.

Diversifying Monetization Strategies

The landscape of monetization is evolving. We'll discuss emerging monetization strategies, from fan subscriptions to non-traditional revenue streams like NFTs, and explore how creators can diversify their income sources for financial stability.

The Influence of AI in Content Recommendations and Creation

Artificial intelligence plays a significant role in content recommendations and creation. We'll discuss the impact of AI algorithms on platform discovery, content personalization, and even AI-generated content, and how creators can adapt to this evolving landscape.

The Role of Ephemeral Content and Short-Form Videos

Ephemeral content and short-form videos capture attention in a fast-paced digital world. We'll explore the appeal of temporary content, platforms like Instagram Stories and TikTok, and strategies for creating engaging short-form content that resonates with modern audiences.

Staying Agile and Adaptable in a Dynamic Environment

The only constant in the digital landscape is change. We'll discuss the importance of staying agile and adaptable as a creator, embracing experimentation, learning from trends, and proactively adjusting your strategies to meet the evolving expectations of your audience.

Collaboration Beyond Platforms: Cross-Media Opportunities

Collaboration extends beyond digital platforms. We'll explore opportunities for cross-media collaborations, including partnerships with traditional media, podcasts, and other mediums, and how creators can leverage these collaborations for expanded reach.

The Future is Yours to Create

In conclusion, the future of content creation is dynamic, filled with possibilities, and yours to create. By staying informed about emerging trends, embracing new technologies, and adapting your strategies, you position yourself not just as a creator of the present but as a visionary shaping the content landscape of the future. As you navigate this ever-evolving journey, remember that your creativity, adaptability, and connection with your audience are the driving forces that will continue to propel your success in the exciting world of online content creation.

Chapter 12: Sustaining Passion and Purpose

Beyond the strategies and trends, sustaining a long and fulfilling journey as a content creator requires a deep connection to your passion and purpose. In this chapter, we'll explore the importance of maintaining authenticity, finding purpose in your content, and fostering a sustainable creative mindset.

The Heart of Your Content: Passion

Passion is the driving force behind your creativity. We'll explore the significance of passion in content creation, how it fuels your commitment to your channel, and strategies for staying connected to the core reasons you started creating content in the first place.

Authenticity as a Cornerstone

Authenticity is your unique fingerprint as a creator. We'll discuss the value of staying true to yourself, how authenticity resonates with audiences, and strategies for maintaining your genuine voice amidst the pressures of the online world.

Aligning Content with Personal Values

Your personal values shape the content you create. We'll explore the importance of aligning your content with your values, how this authenticity attracts like-minded audiences, and strategies for staying true to your principles in a constantly evolving landscape.

Finding Purpose Beyond Metrics

While metrics are essential, purpose goes beyond numbers. We'll discuss how to define your purpose as a creator, the role it plays in sustaining motivation, and strategies for infusing purpose into your content to create a meaningful impact.

Balancing Passion and Practicality

Balancing passion with practical considerations is a common challenge. We'll explore strategies for navigating the intersection of passion and practicality, including time management, setting realistic goals, and finding harmony between your creative pursuits and other life responsibilities.

Embracing Evolution Without Losing Essence

As your content evolves, it's crucial to retain your essence. We'll discuss the balance between growth and authenticity, strategies for evolving your content while staying true to your core identity, and how this evolution contributes to long-term sustainability.

Nurturing a Positive Creator Mindset

A positive mindset is the foundation of resilience. We'll explore strategies for nurturing a positive creator mindset, handling setbacks with grace, and developing mental resilience to navigate the challenges inherent in the creative journey.

Cultivating a Healthy Relationship with Feedback

Feedback is a valuable tool for growth. We'll discuss how to cultivate a healthy relationship with feedback, separating constructive criticism from negativity, and leveraging feedback as a means of continuous improvement.

Mindful Self-Care in a Digital Landscape

Digital spaces can be demanding, and self-care is crucial. We'll explore the importance of mindful self-care, establishing boundaries, and strategies for maintaining a healthy balance between your online presence and your well-being.

Fostering Connections Within the Creator Community

The creator community is a source of support and inspiration. We'll discuss the benefits of fostering connections within the creator community, collaborating, sharing experiences, and creating a network that enhances your sense of belonging in the creative space.

Acknowledging and Celebrating Milestones

Celebrating milestones is essential for motivation. We'll explore the importance of acknowledging and celebrating your achievements, whether big or small, and how these moments contribute to a positive and fulfilling creator journey.

Adapting to Change with Grace

Change is inevitable, and adapting gracefully is a skill. We'll discuss strategies for embracing change, navigating uncertainties, and finding strength in your ability to adapt to the evolving landscape of content creation.

Reflecting on Your Creative Journey

Reflection is a powerful tool for growth. We'll explore the benefits of regularly reflecting on your creative journey, learning from experiences, and using insights gained to shape the direction of your content and your overall approach as a creator.

The Everlasting Fuel: Passion and Purpose

In conclusion, passion and purpose are the everlasting fuel that sustains your journey as a content creator. As you navigate the dynamic landscape of online content creation, always return to the core of why you started, the authenticity that sets you apart, and the purpose that propels your content forward. Your passion and purpose are not just guiding lights; they are the essence that makes your creative journey fulfilling, sustainable, and uniquely yours. May your continued exploration and expression through your content bring you joy, fulfillment, and a lasting impact on the communities you touch.

Chapter 13: Legacy Building and Giving Back

As you continue your journey as a content creator, the concept of legacy becomes increasingly significant. This chapter explores the idea of leaving a lasting impact, giving back to your community, and building a legacy that extends beyond your content.

Defining Your Creator Legacy

Your legacy is the mark you leave on the digital landscape. We'll explore the concept of a creator legacy, how it transcends metrics and views, and the significance of consciously shaping the narrative of your impact as a content creator.

Creating Evergreen Content with Lasting Value

Evergreen content stands the test of time. We'll discuss the importance of creating content with lasting value, how to identify evergreen topics within your niche, and strategies for ensuring your content remains relevant long into the future.

Building a Sustainable Brand Identity

Your brand identity is a cornerstone of your legacy. We'll explore strategies for building a sustainable brand, from consistent visual elements to a cohesive message, and how a strong brand identity contributes to a memorable and impactful legacy.

Giving Back to Your Community

Community support is fundamental to your success. We'll discuss ways to give back to your community, whether through special content, community engagement initiatives, or support for charitable causes, and how this commitment strengthens your creator legacy.

Mentoring and Supporting Emerging Creators

Mentorship is a powerful way to leave a positive impact. We'll explore the benefits of mentoring emerging creators, sharing your knowledge and experiences, and how this contributes to a culture of support within the broader creator community.

Documenting Your Creative Journey

Documenting your journey adds depth to your legacy. We'll discuss the importance of sharing behind-the-scenes insights, lessons learned, and the evolution of your content, creating a narrative that resonates with both longtime fans and new audiences.

Hosting Educational and Inspirational Content

Educational and inspirational content has enduring appeal. We'll explore how to integrate educational elements into your content, share insights from your journey, and inspire others by showcasing both successes and challenges.

Cultivating Positive Online Spaces

Creating a positive online space is part of your legacy. We'll discuss strategies for fostering a welcoming and inclusive environment within your community, mitigating negativity, and building a digital space that reflects your values.

Collaborating on Impactful Projects

Collaborations can amplify your impact. We'll explore how collaborating on impactful projects, whether with other creators or organizations, allows you to leverage collective efforts for social good and leaves a lasting legacy of positive change.

Supporting Social Causes and Philanthropy

Engaging in social causes adds depth to your legacy. We'll discuss ways to support social causes and incorporate philanthropy into your content, contributing to meaningful change and aligning your legacy with values of social responsibility.

Diversifying Content for Varied Audiences

Diversifying your content expands your reach. We'll explore strategies for creating content that appeals to varied audiences, ensuring that your legacy resonates with people from different backgrounds, interests, and perspectives.

Documenting Personal Growth and Reflections

Personal growth is a key component of your legacy. We'll discuss the value of documenting your own growth, sharing reflections on your creative journey, and how this vulnerability and authenticity connect with your audience on a deeper level.

Creating Timeless and Impactful Projects

Timeless projects leave an enduring mark. We'll explore how to conceptualize and execute projects that transcend trends, making a lasting impact and contributing to a legacy that stands the test of time.

Engaging with Fans and Building a Community Archive

Engaging with your fans creates a sense of community. We'll discuss strategies for building a community archive, showcasing fan contributions, and how these interactions become part of the collective memory of your creator legacy.

Planning for the Future: Succession and Transition

Planning for the future is a responsible approach to legacy building. We'll explore considerations for succession and transition, whether passing the reins to a new creator or planning for the continuation of your brand beyond your active involvement.

Your Legacy, Your Impact

In conclusion, your legacy as a content creator is a culmination of the impact you've had on your audience, your community, and the digital landscape. As you consciously shape and build your legacy, remember that it's not just about the content you create but the positive influence you leave behind. Your legacy is a living testament to the connections you've forged, the support you've given, and the lasting mark you've made on the world of online content creation. May your legacy continue to inspire and resonate, leaving a positive and enduring imprint for generations to come.

Chapter 14: Reflections and Continued Growth

As your journey as a content creator unfolds, reflection becomes a valuable tool for continued growth. This chapter delves into the importance of reflection, strategies for ongoing improvement, and the mindset required to adapt and thrive in the ever-evolving landscape of online content creation.

The Art of Reflection

Reflection is a powerful mechanism for growth. We'll explore the art of reflection, including the benefits of looking back on your journey, learning from experiences, and using insights gained to refine your content and strategies.

Celebrating Milestones and Acknowledging Achievements

Milestones are markers of your progress. We'll discuss the significance of celebrating milestones, both big and small, acknowledging your achievements, and how these moments of reflection contribute to a positive creator mindset.

Learning from Setbacks and Challenges

Setbacks are opportunities for learning. We'll explore strategies for navigating challenges, viewing setbacks as stepping stones to improvement, and how resilience in the face of adversity is a hallmark of successful content creators.

Adapting to Viewer Feedback and Changing Trends

Viewer feedback is a valuable resource. We'll discuss strategies for interpreting and adapting to feedback, staying attuned to changing viewer preferences and industry trends, and how this responsiveness contributes to the ongoing relevance of your content.

Balancing Consistency and Evolution

Consistency and evolution coexist in successful channels. We'll explore the delicate balance between maintaining a consistent content schedule and allowing room for evolution, ensuring that your channel stays fresh while still delivering what your audience expects.

Nurturing a Growth Mindset

A growth mindset is foundational for continuous improvement. We'll discuss the characteristics of a growth mindset, strategies for cultivating it, and how this mindset fosters a dynamic and evolving approach to content creation.

Experimentation and Trying New Ideas

Experimentation is key to staying innovative. We'll explore the importance of trying new ideas, whether it's experimenting with content formats, exploring new platforms, or incorporating fresh elements into your videos to keep your content dynamic.

Staying Informed About Industry Trends

Staying informed is a creator's responsibility. We'll discuss the importance of keeping abreast of industry trends, technological advancements, and shifts in viewer behavior, and how this awareness positions you to proactively adapt to the changing landscape.

Refining Your Brand and Channel Identity

Brand identity is a living entity. We'll explore strategies for refining your brand and channel identity over time, ensuring that it continues to align with your evolving content, values, and the expectations of your growing audience.

Adopting New Technologies and Platforms

Embracing new technologies is part of staying relevant. We'll discuss the role of emerging technologies in content creation, from adopting new features on existing platforms to exploring entirely new platforms that align with your content and audience.

Engaging with Your Community Through Feedback Loops

Creating feedback loops enhances community engagement. We'll explore strategies for actively engaging with your audience, seeking feedback, and creating a dialogue that not only strengthens your community but also provides valuable insights for your creative decisions.

Setting and Reevaluating Goals Periodically

Goals are guideposts for growth. We'll discuss the importance of setting clear and measurable goals, periodically evaluating your progress, and how this goal-oriented approach provides a roadmap for the continued success of your channel.

Diversifying Content Without Losing Focus

Diversification is a form of expansion. We'll explore how to diversify your content without losing focus, ensuring that new content strands complement your core identity and resonate with your audience while expanding your creative horizons.

Building a Long-Term Content Strategy

Long-term success requires a strategic approach. We'll discuss the elements of building a long-term content strategy, including planning for sustained growth, staying adaptable to change, and the iterative nature of refining your strategy over time.

Cultivating a Healthy Work-Life-Creation Balance

Balance is crucial for sustainable content creation. We'll explore strategies for maintaining a healthy work-life-creation balance, preventing burnout, and ensuring that your passion for creating content remains a sustainable and fulfilling endeavor.

Expressing Gratitude to Your Audience

Gratitude is a powerful mindset. We'll discuss the importance of expressing gratitude to your audience, whether through dedicated content, community interactions, or gestures of appreciation, and how this gratitude fosters a positive creator-audience relationship.

Continuing the Journey: Forever a Creator

In conclusion, the journey of a content creator is an ongoing adventure. As you reflect on your path, celebrate achievements, and learn from experiences, remember that the essence of being a creator is the continuous pursuit of improvement and innovation. Embrace the ever-evolving nature of online content creation, stay true to your passion, and continue to thrive as a creator who leaves a lasting impact on the digital landscape. Your journey is a testament to the dynamic and creative spirit that defines the world of content creation. Here's to the next chapter of your endless journey as a creator!

Chapter 15: A Future Unwritten

As you stand at the threshold of what lies ahead, this chapter invites you to contemplate the unwritten chapters of your creative journey. The future is a canvas waiting for your strokes, and this chapter explores the possibilities, aspirations, and the endless potential that awaits you as a content creator.

The Blank Canvas of Tomorrow

The future is your blank canvas. We'll delve into the excitement of the unknown, the potential for innovation, and the joy of exploring uncharted territories in the dynamic landscape of content creation.

Aspirations and Goals for the Future

As you peer into the future, what are your aspirations? We'll discuss setting new goals, envisioning the milestones you aim to achieve, and the thrill of embarking on projects that challenge and inspire you.

Adapting to Technological Advancements

Technology is a driving force in the digital realm. We'll explore how staying at the forefront of technological advancements can open new avenues for your content, from immersive experiences to cutting-edge production techniques.

Navigating Changes in Audience Behavior

Audience behaviors evolve, and so must your content strategy. We'll discuss strategies for staying attuned to changes in viewer preferences, adapting to shifts in how audiences consume content, and remaining relevant in a constantly changing landscape.

Exploring Emerging Platforms and Trends

New platforms and trends emerge, offering fresh opportunities. We'll explore the excitement of venturing into unexplored platforms, experimenting with emerging content formats, and how staying abreast of trends can keep your content on the cutting edge.

Global Reach and Cultural Impact

The digital world knows no boundaries. We'll discuss the potential for global reach, the impact your content can have across diverse cultures, and how embracing a global audience enriches your creative experience.

Innovative Collaborations and Partnerships

Collaborations are windows to new possibilities. We'll explore the potential for innovative collaborations and partnerships, pushing the boundaries of what can be achieved when creative minds come together.

The Role of AI and Automation in Content Creation

Artificial intelligence and automation are transforming content creation. We'll discuss the evolving role of AI in areas like content recommendations, creation assistance, and the ways in which automation can enhance your workflow.

Sustainability in Content Creation

Sustainability is an increasingly important consideration. We'll explore how creators can contribute to a sustainable digital environment, whether through eco-conscious content or by promoting sustainable practices within the community.

Expanding Monetization Strategies

Monetization avenues are diversifying. We'll discuss emerging opportunities, from non-fungible tokens (NFTs) to innovative membership models, and how creators can strategically expand their monetization strategies for financial resilience.

The Intersection of Entertainment and Education

The boundaries between entertainment and education continue to blur. We'll explore the potential for creating content that entertains while imparting knowledge, contributing to a culture of lifelong learning in your audience.

Cultivating a Community of Impact

Your community is the heart of your journey. We'll explore how cultivating a community of impact goes beyond numbers, focusing on meaningful interactions, shared experiences, and the positive influence your community can have on the broader digital landscape.

The Joy of Experimentation and Playfulness

Never lose the joy of experimentation. We'll discuss the importance of playfulness in your creative process, embracing experimentation as a source of inspiration, and the delight that comes from pushing the boundaries of your creativity.

Mindful Content Creation in a Noisy World

In a world filled with content, mindfulness stands out. We'll explore the significance of creating content with intention, cutting through the noise to deliver messages that resonate with authenticity and purpose.

Building a Lasting Creator Legacy

Your legacy is an ongoing narrative. We'll discuss how to shape a lasting creator legacy, not just through content but by contributing to the wider creative community, inspiring future creators, and leaving an indelible mark on the world of online content.

The Endless Journey Continues

As this chapter unfolds, so does your unwritten future. The endless journey of a content creator is a tapestry of creativity, innovation, and connection. With each stroke of your creativity, you're not just shaping content; you're crafting a legacy. Here's to the unwritten chapters, the unexplored horizons, and the boundless possibilities that await you in the ever-evolving adventure of content creation. May your future be as vibrant and limitless as your imagination.

Conclusion

As we reach the conclusion of this journey through the world of content creation, it's essential to reflect on the profound impact you, as a content creator, can have on the digital landscape. Your journey is not merely about creating videos; it's a dynamic exploration of passion, creativity, and connection.

From the foundational steps of finding your niche to the intricacies of building a sustainable brand, you've embraced the challenges and celebrated the triumphs that define the creator's path. You've navigated the ever-shifting algorithms, stayed resilient in the face of challenges, and cultivated a community that finds value in your unique voice.

The chapters have unfolded like seasons, each bringing its own lessons and opportunities for growth. You've explored the art of storytelling, mastered the tools of your trade, and embraced the duality of passion and practicality. Along the way, you've not only crafted content but shaped a legacy that extends beyond the screen.

The future, as outlined in the last chapter, is an unwritten canvas awaiting your strokes. Technological advancements, emerging platforms, and evolving audience behaviors present exciting possibilities. As you stand on the cusp of the unknown, remember that your creativity knows no bounds.

Continue to set aspirational goals, experiment with new ideas, and stay mindful of the impact you can have. Whether through educational content that enlightens or entertaining narratives that captivate, your role as a content creator extends beyond entertainment; it's about making a meaningful contribution to the digital landscape.

In every setback, find a lesson. In every success, find inspiration. Your journey is a testament to the ever-evolving nature of content creation, and the story you tell is

not just your own; it resonates with audiences who find solace, inspiration, and connection in your creations.

As you venture into the unwritten future, may your creativity soar, your community thrive, and your legacy endure. This is not just a conclusion; it's an invitation to continue shaping the narrative of your creative journey, for there are always new stories to tell, new milestones to achieve, and new chapters waiting to be written.

Thank you for embarking on this journey. Here's to the boundless possibilities that lie ahead and the endless creativity that defines your role as a content creator. The canvas is yours—paint boldly.